Resource Book for Primary Students

New Edition

Esme Ettershank and Robyn Conlin

Table of Contents

English

The *Australian Curriculum: English* is based on three integrated strands. These three strands are essential for students to fully develop their understanding of the English language, and how they use it in a range of contexts throughout their life.

The three strands are:

Language

This is understanding the English language and how it works. The Language strand includes the concepts of punctuation, spelling and grammar.

Literature

This is appreciating the English language. The Literature strand includes the study of books and authors to develop literary appreciation.

Literacy

This is developing a range of uses for the English language. The Literacy strand includes the study of a variety of text types and a range of genres, so that students are aware of the potential of written and spoken language for different purposes.

Language

Punctuation

We need to use proper punctuation so that our writing can be easily understood by readers. The following text presents some of the most common punctuation marks used in writing, including examples of when they are used.

Full Stop   (.)

A full stop is used:

- to mark the end of a sentence

- after abbreviations

    etc.   cont.   i.e.   e.g.

Abbreviations ending in the final letter of the original word do not need a full stop.

    St (Street), Qld (Queensland), Mr (Mister), Dr (Doctor)

No full stop is used after the symbols for metric measures.

    10 cm, 250 g, 100 mL

Most acronyms (words that are made by using the first letter of each word in a group of words) do not use full stops.

    NSW, SA, WA, USA

Capital Letters (A, B, C)

A capital letter is used for:

- the first word in a sentence

- the pronoun 'I'

- the first word in direct speech
    George whispered, "Watch out for the trick question."

- the first letter in an abbreviation
    St (Street), Qld (Queensland), Mr (Mister), Dr (Doctor)

- each letter in an acronym
    RSVP, CSIRO, USA, NSW, ANZAC, ASAP

- the first letter in a proper noun (proper nouns are the names of people, places, months, days, etc.)
    David, Ann, Indonesia, September, Friday

- the first letter in the main words in titles of books, poems, songs, etc.
    The Hobbit, 'Advance Australia Fair'

- the first word of special titles
    the Prime Minister, the Governor-General

Question Mark (?)

A question mark is used:

- to mark the end of a question in direct speech
    Ella asked her mother, "Can I go for a swim?"

- when a question is implied
    This afternoon?

Apostrophe (')

An apostrophe is used to show:

- that one or more letters have been left out in contractions
    hasn't (has not), it's (it is)

- possession or ownership
    a girl's pencil, two boys' hats, Ann's dog

Where to place the apostrophe to show ownership:

Write the owner(s):	a girl	two girls
Add an apostrophe:	a girl'	two girls'
Add 's' if it is needed:	a girl's pencil	two girls' pencils

When to use 'it's' or 'its':

If you can substitute 'it is' for 'it's' in a sentence, then the contraction 'it's' is correct.

> If it's still raining, we will go by car.　√
>
> If it is still raining, we will go by car.　√

'Its' shows ownership; you can't substitute 'it is', so 'its' is correct.

> The dog ate all the food in its bowl.　√
>
> The dog ate all the food in it is bowl.　✗

Comma　(,)

A comma is used:

- to show you where to pause when reading a sentence aloud

- to separate words in a list (but no comma is needed before 'and' in a list)

  > Tony, Jack, Matt and Vanh all went swimming.

- after words such as 'however' and 'perhaps' if they interrupt the main idea being expressed

  > The next time you come, however, you will bring your own pencil.

- to separate phrases or clauses in a sentence

  > By following the dog, the girls soon found the missing treasure.
  >
  > After they had found the lost child, the searchers all returned to camp.

- to show a word, phrase or clause that gives extra information

  > My youngest sister, Sally, is a clever storyteller.
  >
  > Mr Bellas, who is 90 years old today, still surfs every morning.

- to introduce direct speech

  > The boy's mother said, "Be careful when you cross the road."

Quotation Marks　(' '/" ")

Quotation marks are used:

- to show direct speech, i.e. the exact words of the speaker

  > Jason said, "John, will you be my partner for this game of tennis?"
  >
  > "Are you sure," asked Jan, "that you have the right book?"

- when quoting text from another source

  > According to the Bible, "Blessed are the merciful".

- for titles of songs and short poems

  > 'Waltzing Matilda', 'The Road to Gundagai'

Titles of books, plays and films are shown in italic type without quotation marks.

> *The Magic Pudding, Doctor Who, Harry Potter and the Philosopher's Stone*

Hyphen   (-)

A hyphen is used:

- when two words are joined to make one word
  starry-eyed, hair-raising, self-confidence

- to avoid confusion in some words with a prefix
  co-author, re-entry, co-worker

- in numbers
  We went to Grandma's fifty-third birthday.

- to break up a word if it will not fit on one line
  They use their tails for bal-
  ancing as they climb up.

Exclamation mark   (!)

An exclamation mark is used:

- after a word, phrase or sentence that expresses strong feeling
  Oh dear!
  Sit down now!
  It's really hot today!
  Yes! I must go with you!

Dash   (–)

A dash is used:

- to show a break in a sentence
  "I don't think –" the trainee pilot began. "You have to do it," interrupted the flying instructor.
  I would buy that car today – if only I had enough money.

- instead of 'to' when placed between numbers
  Australians fought in World War II (1939–45)

- to show an extra thought or an 'aside'
  To do this correctly – as you are aware – you will need to be very precise in your measurements.

A pair of commas or brackets could be used above instead of the dashes.

Brackets   ( )

Brackets (also called 'parentheses') are used:

- to show a word, phrase or clause that gives extra information
  Mt Kosciuszko (2228 metres) is the highest mountain in Australia.

- to show the source of a quotation or piece of information

    I believe that all people should have to vote in elections (Tom Wing – Year 8)

Square brackets can be used inside the first set of brackets if two sets of brackets are needed in one sentence. They are also used to show an editor's note or extra information.

    Mt Kosciuszko is the highest point in Australia. (Lake Eyre [at 15 metres below sea level] is the lowest.)

    "It [the accident] was terrible," said the witness.

Braces can be used to show a set of choices or to show a set of numbers in mathematics.

    Choose a colour {pink, purple, yellow, blue} to complete the picture.

Semicolon   (;)

A semicolon is used:

- to link two ideas in a sentence that are not joined by a conjunction

    The marathon runner was almost exhausted; she struggled on towards the finishing line.

- in a list of items where commas are already being used

    For this experiment, you will need a 2.5 m piece of string; a pencil, paper and ruler; a stopwatch, with a memory function; and a metal mass.

Colon   (:)

A colon is used:

- to separate an introduction from the details that follow

    She can speak five languages: English, French, German, Japanese and Italian.

- to introduce items in a list

    You will need:

    3 eggs

    1 cup flour

    1 cup milk

Spelling

It is important to know about words, and also to know how to learn new words. You also need to know how to check the spelling of words you are trying to write. There are four ways of understanding how words are spelt:

Visual

This is using your memory of how a word looks.

Phonological

This is using sound–letter relationships.

Morphological

This is using parts of words to build word families.

Etymological

This is using word origins and derivations.

Plurals

Nouns, pronouns and other parts of speech can be singular (showing one only) or plural (showing more than one).

Most nouns form the plural by adding 's' to the singular.

desk → desks

Nouns ending in 'y' preceded by a consonant form the plural by changing 'y' into 'i' and adding 'es'.

baby → babies

Nouns ending in 'y' preceded by a vowel form the plural by adding 's'.

monkey → monkeys

Nouns ending in 'ch', 's', 'sh' or 'x' form the plural by adding 'es'.

church → churches; moss → mosses; rash → rashes; box → boxes

Exception: stomach → stomachs

Some nouns ending in 'f' or 'fe' change to 've' before adding 's' to form the plural.

calf → calves; knife → knives

Exception: 'wharf' can be 'wharfs' or 'wharves'; 'dwarf' can be 'dwarfs' or 'dwarves'; 'roof' can be 'roofs' or 'rooves'

Most nouns ending in the long 'o' sound preceded by a consonant form the plural by adding 'es'.

tomato → tomatoes

Exceptions: memos, photos, pianos, radios, silos, solos

Some nouns form the plural by a change of a vowel or vowels.

tooth → teeth; goose → geese; axis → axes; man → men; woman → women

Some nouns have the same form in the singular and the plural.

bream, cod, deer, dozen, innings, reindeer, salmon, sheep, trout

Some nouns have no singular form.

billiards, forceps, gallows, pants, pliers, scissors, tongs, trousers, tweezers

English

Contractions

Contractions occur when two words are joined together to make one word.
An apostrophe is used to show missing letters.

Extended Form	Contraction	Extended Form	Contraction
did not	didn't	I am	I'm
are not	aren't	you are	you're
does not	doesn't	he is	he's
has not	hasn't	she is	she's
can not	can't	we are	we're
let us	let's	they are	they're

Misspelt Words

The following words are often spelt incorrectly. When in doubt about a word, take time to check this list. We can also use a dictionary, a thesaurus or spell check – if working on a computer – to check our spelling.

accommodation	disappear	impostor	receive
ache	disappoint	independent	recipe
adviser	disease	instead	restaurant
again	early	interesting	schedule
already	eighth	jewellery	separate
always	embarrass	journal	sergeant
among	enough	knew	shoulder
answer	entrance	knock	skilful
beautiful	except	known	souvenir
because	experience	machinery	stomach
believe	families	meant	straight
biscuit	February	medicine	successful
breakfast	finally	mischievous	sufficient
built	fortunately	nearly	supervisor
burglar	friend	neighbour	suppose
business	front	neither	tendency
caught	fulfil	nephew	terrible
chief	government	occasion	together
choose	guard	occurred	tough
climbed	guessed	orchestra	trouble
cough	handkerchief	parallel	truly
could	haven't	piece	umbrella
crept	heard	practically	unconscious
damage	heavy	precede	usually
definite	height	preferred	whose
describe	hospital	preparation	wonderful
development	imaginary	proceed	written
difference	immediately	ready	yacht

The verb and noun forms of these words have different spellings:
advice (noun), advise (verb)
licence (noun), license (verb)
practice (noun), practise (verb)

Suffixes

Adding '-ed', '-ing'
Add '-ed' or '-ing' to the base word:
> jump → jumped; fly → flying

When a word has one syllable with a single vowel followed by a single consonant, double the last consonant before adding '-ed' or '-ing':
> stop → stopped; run → running

A word ending in 'ee' retains the 'ee' when adding '-ing':
> agreeing, fleeing, guaranteeing, refereeing, seeing

When a word ends in a silent 'e', drop the 'e' before adding '-ing':
> shave → shaving

Exceptions: canoeing, dyeing, glueing, singeing, tiptoeing, whingeing

Adding '-able', '-ous'
When a word ends in a silent 'e', drop the 'e' before adding '-able' or '-ous':
> desire → desirable; desire → desirous

When a word ends in '-ce' or '-ge', retain the 'e' when adding '-able' or '-ous':
> notice → noticeable; courage → courageous

Adding '-ly', '-ment'
Do not drop the silent letter 'e' when adding '-ly' or '-ment':
> sincere → sincerely; amaze → amazement

Exceptions: due → duly, true → truly, argue → argument

Adding '-er'
Add '-er' to the base word:
> teach → teacher; employ → employer

When a word has one syllable with a single vowel followed by a single consonant, double the last consonant before adding '-er':
> run → runner; big → bigger

When a word already ends in 'e', add '-r':
> bake → baker

Adding '-est'
Add '-est' to the base word:
> small → smallest

When a word has one syllable with a single vowel followed by a single consonant, double the last consonant before adding '-est':

> big → biggest

Adding '-full'

Add '-full' to the base word then drop the last 'l':

> help → helpful; skill → skillful

Homographs

Homographs are words that have the same spelling but different meanings.
They are sometimes pronounced differently too. To work out the appropriate meaning and pronunciation of the word, you need to understand the context it is being used in.

saw → observed	saw → a tool to cut wood	
wind → breeze	wind → turn	
wound → injury	wound → turned	
lead → a dog's lead	lead → a kind of metal	lead → to direct

Homophones

Homophones are words that sound the same but have different spelling and meanings.

sew → to stitch	sow → to plant seeds
affect → to cause change	effect → the result
lightening → making lighter	lightning → a bolt of electricity
aloud → audible	allowed → permitted
loose → not tight	lose → to misplace
complement → to complete or go well with	compliment → praise
pedalling → riding a bicycle	peddling → selling
dual → with two	duel → a fight between two people
principal → the chief person	principle → a premise or belief
dyeing → changing colour	dying → ceasing to live
stationary → not moving	stationery → writing materials
weather → climate	whether → whether or not
you're → you are	your → belonging to you

their → belonging to them	there → a position or the beginning of a statement of fact	they're → they are
wear → to wear clothes	where → a question of location	we're → we are
rein → a tool to help steer a horse	reign → to rule	rain → wet weather

poor → not rich   paw → a dog's foot   pour → to pour liquid   pore → an opening in the skin

Sentences

A sentence is a complete thought expressed in words. It must make sense. A sentence may:

* state a fact

    The mouse scampered away.

* give an order

    Catch the ball, Kate.

- ask a question

  Why did you go that way?

- make an exclamation

  That kite flew so high!

Single words or groups of words can be added to a sentence to give extra information, or to add to the meaning of the sentence.

Phrases

A phrase is a group of words that does not make sense by itself. A phrase can act like an adjective or adverb – it adds information to a verb or a noun.

A phrase usually begins with a preposition.

The flowers <u>on that bush</u> have a strong perfume.

('on that bush' is an adjectival phrase describing 'flowers')

The three children dived <u>into the swimming pool.</u>

('into the swimming pool' is an adverbial phrase telling where they dived)

Some phrases include a verb.

<u>Bowling accurately</u>, Jason soon had the batsman out.

Jenny's team needed three more goals <u>to win the match</u>.

Clauses

A clause is a group of words that includes a verb.

A dependent clause does not make sense by itself – it needs a main clause for the sentence to make sense.

I included all those <u>who could catch a ball</u> in the team.

An independent clause makes sense by itself.

I included all of them in the team because <u>they could all catch the ball</u>.

An adjectival clause adds information about a noun.

The ball <u>that John brought to school</u> was used to play football.

('that John brought to school' tells more about the ball)

An adverbial clause adds information about a verb.

<u>While she was walking through the park</u>, Ann found an injured bird.

('while she was walking through the park' tells when Ann found the bird)

Sometimes two short sentences can be combined into a longer, more interesting sentence using a clause.

The boy was lost in the bush.

He became afraid as night approached.

→ As night approached, the boy who was lost in the bush became afraid.

Simple Sentences

A simple sentence contains one complete thought with only one verb.

They were playing with the football.

Complex Sentences

A complex sentence contains two or more clauses. The principal (or main) clause makes sense on its own. The subordinate clause does not make sense on its own. It needs the principal clause for the sentence to be complete.

Because it was a rainy day, the children stayed in their classroom.

('the children stayed in their classroom' is a principal clause and 'Because it was a rainy day' is the subordinate clause)

Compound Sentences

A compound sentence has two or more principal clauses, each of which makes sense on its own. They are joined by a conjunction.

The little boy ran into the room but he did not disturb the sleeping baby.

('The little boy ran into the room' is a principal clause, 'he did not disturb the sleeping baby' is a principal clause and 'but' is the conjunction that joins these two clauses)

Grammar

When a word is classified according to its use in a sentence, we can identify it as a particular part of speech. However, it is possible for a word to be classified one way in one sentence, and classified differently in another sentence. Each word must be analysed and classified according to how it is used in a particular sentence.

Jill had a <u>round</u> bowl for her salad. (adjective)

Dad will <u>round</u> up the cows ready for milking. (verb)

He looked <u>around</u> but could not see his brother. (adverb)

We ran <u>around</u> the paddock trying to catch the horse. (preposition)

Nouns

A noun is a word that names an animal, person, place or thing.

Common nouns are general words that name animals, people, places and things.

cow, farmer, village, city, ball

Proper nouns name particular people, places, days and months.

Robert, Melbourne, Tuesday, July, the Prime Minister of Australia

Collective nouns name groups of animals, people and things.

bunch, gang, class, army

Abstract nouns name things that cannot be seen, heard or touched, such as ideas and feelings.

happiness, poverty, danger, love

Pronouns

A pronoun is a word that can be used instead of a noun.

<u>She</u> sailed the boat on the lake.

('She' is the pronoun)

The following words are pronouns:

- I, me, my, myself, mine

- we, us, our, ourselves, ours

- you, your, yours, yourself, yourselves

- he, him, his, himself

- she, her, hers, herself

- they, them, their, theirs, themselves

- it, its, itself

Pronouns never take an apostrophe to show ownership.

Adjectives

An adjective is a describing word that gives extra information about a noun or pronoun. An adjective tells:

- what sort

The <u>lazy</u> boy did not come.

- how much

They needed the <u>whole</u> roll of paper.

- how many

<u>Several</u> girls played netball.

- which

<u>Those</u> children are nearly finished.

An adjective usually comes before the noun it is describing, but sometimes it follows the noun if a verb is used.

We eat the <u>juicy</u> apples.

The apples are <u>juicy</u> so we eat them.

When comparing two nouns, add '-er' to the adjective or use 'more' (for longer words).

> This puzzle is <u>easier</u> than the last one we tried.
>
> A diamond is <u>more precious</u> than a topaz.

When comparing more than two things, add '-est' to the adjective or use 'most' (for longer words).

> This stick is the <u>shortest</u> of them all.
>
> Melissa was voted the <u>most popular</u> person in the class.

Some adjectives form irregular comparisons.

> bad → worse → worst,   many → more → most,   good → better → best

Some adjectives cannot form comparisons.

> perfect, empty, full, unique

Verbs

A verb is an action word. A sentence must contain at least one verb.

A verb can tell how something is done (a 'doing' word).

> The jet <u>flew</u> across the sky.

A verb can show a state of being ('being' words: am, are, is, was, were, be, been, being).

> Tanya <u>is</u> a good swimmer.

A verb can show ownership ('having' words: has, had, have, having).

> Jonathan <u>has</u> many marbles.

While many of the 'being' and 'having' words can be verbs on their own, they are often used with another verb to form a compound verb. When they are used this way, they are called 'auxiliary verbs'.

> The bees <u>are swarming</u> around the hive.
>
> The boys <u>have found</u> the missing football.
>
> They <u>have been swimming</u> in the pool.
>
> The children <u>can follow</u> the track through the forest.

Adverbs

An adverb is a word that adds meaning to a verb by telling how, when or where something is done. It can also add meaning to adjective or another adverb.

> The old man ate <u>slowly</u>. (how)
>
> Our cousins arrived <u>yesterday</u>. (when)
>
> The kitten scampered <u>upstairs</u>. (where)

Words such as 'very' and 'rather' are also adverbs.

> The pianist played a <u>very</u> tuneful piece. (how tuneful)
>
> She sang <u>rather</u> softly. (how softly)

The word 'not' is an adverb. It is never part of a verb, even when it is placed between two parts of a compound verb.

> The aircraft <u>was</u> not <u>flying</u> on the correct route.

Prepositions

A preposition introduces a phrase. A phrase adds extra information to a sentence, like an adjective or an adverb.

> The men were rescued <u>from their sinking boat</u>.

> **('from' is a preposition and 'from their sinking boat' is an adverbial phrase, telling from where they were rescued)**

Some common prepositions are:

> on, at, in, up, near, with, between, among, into, down, by, from, during, towards, above

Conjunctions

A conjunction is a word that joins two words, phrases or clauses.

> John brought his pen <u>and</u> pencil with him.
>
> You will find your ball in the basket <u>or</u> in the box.
>
> Sarah and Jane are playing netball, <u>but</u> Farrah and Amy are playing softball.

A conjunction can also be placed at the beginning of a sentence.

> <u>If</u> you tell him now, he will come.

Some common conjunctions are:

> and, but, or, because, as, unless, while, although, if, where

Relative Pronouns

A relative pronoun joins two clauses and replaces a noun at the same time.

Some relative pronouns are:

> who, whose, whom, that, which

A relative pronoun introduces an adjectival clause, and follows the noun or pronoun to which it refers.

> Those are the eggs <u>that</u> we collected from the henhouse.
>
> He is the man <u>who</u> broke into the house.

Participles

A participle is a word that is part verb and part adjective.

The present participle always ends in '-ing'.

> The driver who was <u>speeding</u> around the corner lost control of the car.

The past participle often ends in '-n', '-en', '-ed', '-d' or '-t'.

> The <u>broken</u> bicycle could not be repaired.

A participle cannot be a verb by itself, but it is often used with an auxiliary verb to form a compound verb.

> George <u>is driving</u> to Canberra but Helen <u>is flying</u>.
> The injured sailor <u>was flown</u> to hospital.

Sometimes a participle introduces a phrase (called a 'participial phrase').

> The children <u>crossing</u> the street remembered the road safety rules.

Sometimes a participle is used like an adjective.

> This is no <u>laughing</u> matter!

Sometimes a participle is used like a noun.

> He hates <u>swimming</u>.
> I love <u>reading</u>.

Articles

The word 'the' is called a definite article. We use it to refer to a particular thing.

> <u>The</u> cat is playing with the ball that belongs to Sue.

The words 'a' and 'an' are called indefinite articles. We use them when we are not talking about a particular thing.

> <u>A</u> cat is <u>a</u> domestic animal.

Tense

Tense means *time*. Tense is the form of the verb that tells whether something is happening in the past, in the present or in the future.

> I <u>ran</u> fast. (past)
> I <u>run</u> fast. (present)
> I <u>will run</u> fast. (future)

The tense should usually remain the same in a complete sentence.

> When Maria <u>finished</u> her lunch, she <u>ran</u> to the swings.   √
> When Maria <u>finished</u> her lunch, she <u>runs</u> to the swings.   ✗

Sometimes a sentence might contain verbs with two different tenses.

> I <u>know</u> that he <u>will go</u> to town this afternoon.

> **('know' → present, 'will go' → future)**

This table shows the different forms of some common verbs in different tenses.

Present Tense	Past Tense	Present Participle	Past Participle
see (I see)	saw (I saw)	seeing (I am seeing)	seen (I have seen)
begin	began	beginning	begun
bring	brought	bringing	brought
draw	drew	drawing	drawn
drive	drove	driving	driven
fly	flew	flying	flown
forget	forgot	forgetting	forgotten
freeze	froze	freezing	frozen
go	went	going	gone
hide	hid	hiding	hidden
keep	kept	keeping	kept
know	knew	knowing	known
ring	rang	ringing	rung
shake	shook	shaking	shaken
swim	swam	swimming	swum
try	tried	trying	tried

Vocabulary

Many of the words we use today have been in the English language for over a thousand years, brought to Britain by the Anglo-Saxons, who gave us the words 'England' and 'English'. Many of our words have come from foreign languages and cultures, and some are derived from the names of people and places. Knowing something about the origins of words can often help us to understand their meanings more fully.

café   French for coffee

cereal   named after Ceres, the Roman goddess of agriculture

dizzy   from the Old English word *dysig* meaning foolish or stupid

evolution   from the Latin word *evolutionem* meaning the unrolling of a book or scroll

humpy	from an Aboriginal word for a bush shelter or *gunyah*
kindergarten	from the German words *kinder* (children) and *garten* (garden)
pasteurisation	the process discovered by Louis Pasteur
robot	from the Czech word *robota* meaning work
google	from the name of the internet search engine Google
bandaid	from the brand name of a product

Latin and Greek Roots

Many English words have developed from Latin and Greek roots. They are called 'roots' because other words 'grow' from them.

Root	Meaning	Derivatives
anima	breath, soul	animal, animate
annus	a year	annual, annuity, biennial
autos	self	autograph, autobiography
bios	life	biology, biography
biblos	a book	bibliography, bible
cado (casus)	I fall	cascade, decay, casually
cedo (cessus)	I go	proceed, exceed, precede
caput (capitis)	the head	capital, captain
chronos	time	chronicle, chronological
colo (cultus)	I till	agriculture, cultivate
cor (cordis)	the heard	cordial, accord, discord
curro (cursus)	I run	current, occurrence, cursive
decem	ten	decimal, December, decimate
dens	teeth	dental, denture, dentist
dico (dictus)	I say	dictate, dictionary, indicate
duco (ductus)	I lead	conduct, education, reduce
facio (factus)	I make	manufacture, defect
linis	the end	final, finite, definite
ge	earth	geography, geology
graphos	drawn or written	autograph, biography, graphic
jacio (jactus)	I throw	eject, interject, reject
locus	a place	local, locality, locate, dislocate
logos	speech, reason	monologue, logic

Root	Meaning	Derivatives
magnus	great	magnificent, magnitude
manus	the hand	manual, manufacture
memor	I remember	memory, remind, memorial
minor	small	minority, minimal, minute
multus	many	multiple, multitude
pono (positus)	I place	deposit, opposition, postpone
populus	the people	popular, population
porto	I carry	portable, transport
struo (structus)	I build	construct, instrument
tele	far	telescope, telegram
tempus	time	temporary, tempo
venio (ventus)	I come	convention, invention, adventure
verto (versus)	I turn	convert, advertise, revert

Latin and Greek Prefixes

A prefix is a syllable placed at the beginning of a word. It changes the meaning of the word. Many antonyms (words with the opposite meaning) are formed by the addition of a prefix.

Prefix	Meaning	Examples
ad-/at-	to	advertise, adventure, attractive
anti-	against	antiseptic, antidote, antitoxin
circum-	around	circumference, circumstance
com-/con-	with, together	combine, companion, consent
de-	down, from	decay, department, deposit
dis-/di-/dif-	away, apart	difference, distribute, diffuse
en-	to make	enlarge, encourage, enslave
ex-	out of	export, exclude, expression
fore-	before	forehead, forecast, forewarn
in-/il-/ir-	not	insoluble, illegal, irresponsible
in-/im-	into	indent, income, import, immigrant
inter-	between	interschool, interrupt, interaction
mid-	middle of	midnight, midstream, midwinter
mis-	wrong	mistake, misbehave, misunderstand

English

Prefix	Meaning	Examples
over-	above	overcast, overestimate, overthrow
post-	after	postscript, postpone, postgraduate
pre-	before	preschool, prepare, prevent
re-	back, again	rewrite, recommend, renew, return
sub-	under	subway, submarine, subject
super-	above	superman, supernatural, supervise
trans-	across	transfer, transport, translate
un-	not	unusual, unequal, unsteady
under-	beneath	underline, underwater, undermine
unus-/monos-	one	universe, unilateral, monologue, monotony
bi-/bis-/duo-	two, twice	bicycle, bisect, bifocal, dual, duel, duet
ter-/tri-	three	triangle, trident, triplet
quadr-/quadri-	four	quadrangle, quadrilateral
penta-	five	pentagon, pentathlon
hexa-	six	hexagon
septem-/hepta-	seven	September, septet, heptagon
octo-	eight	October, octagon, octave
novem-	nine	November
dec-	ten	December, decimal, decathlon
centum-	hundred(th)	centipede, century, centimetre
kilo-	thousand	kilometre, kilogram, kilolitre
milli-	thousand(th)	millipede, millimetre, millilitre

Latin and Greek Suffixes

A suffix is a syllable at the end of a word. It changes the part of speech that the word fits into. The following are some examples of words that contain suffixes.

Suffix	Meaning	Examples
Noun forming:		
-ar/-er/-or	one who	scholar, manager, editor
-ant/-ent	one who	servant, attendant, opponent
-ist	one who	dentist, typist, cyclist

Suffix	Meaning	Examples
-ee	one who is	employee, trainee, referee
-ment/-ness	state of being or doing	enjoyment, loneliness, sickness
-ship/-hood	state of being	championship, apprenticeship, childhood
-ance/-ence	state of being or doing	resemblance, dependence, inference
-ure/-age	state of being or doing	seizure, bondage, breakage
-y/-ity/-ice	state of being	autonomy, minority, service
-ion/-our	act or state of	application, labour, behaviour
-ary/-ery/-ory	place where	library, nursery, directory
-er	one who	singer, trainer, painter
-ism	belief	communism, realism, cubism
-tude	state of	attitude, fortitude, certitude

Adjective forming:

Suffix	Meaning	Examples
-ful/-ous	full of	beautiful, poisonous, awful
-able/-ible	able to be	noticeable, credible, likeable
-less	without	hopeless, careless, homeless
-en	made of	woollen, earthen, golden
-ive/-ar/-ary	relating to	festive, polar, temporary
-ish	like or somewhat	foolish, childish, yellowish
-ly	like	friendly, lonely, fatherly
-al	relating to	dental, essential, oral
-ac/-ic	like, pertaining to	cardiac, aquatic
-escent	becoming	pubescent, fluorescent, evanescent

Adverb forming:

Suffix	Meaning	Examples
-ly	like	continually, angrily, sweetly
-ward/-wards	towards	forwards, backwards, upwards

Verb forming:

Suffix	Meaning	Examples
-en/-ise	to make	darken, advertise, agonise

Collective Nouns

Collective nouns refer to groups of things.

a constellation of stars	a menagerie of animals	a hive of bees
a fleet of ships	a murder of crows	a ream of paper
a bouquet of flowers	a swarm of locusts	a gaggle of geese
a clutch of eggs	a muster of peacocks	a litter of puppies
a leap of leopards	an album of photos	a pod of whales
a pride of lions	a hand of bananas	a grove of trees
a herd of cattle	a host of angels	a cluster of diamonds
a flock of sheep	a brood of chickens	a school of fish
a bunting of flags	a batch of scones	a deck of cards
a board of directors	a bale of turtles	a gang of thieves

Synonyms

A synonym is a word that has the same or a similar meaning as another word.

quick → fast; happy → cheerful; sad → miserable

Word	Synonym	Word	Synonym
aim	purpose	holiday	vacation
ban	prohibit	huge	immense
basis	foundation	large	extensive
brave	courageous	necessary	essential
careful	cautious	practise	rehearse
collect	accumulate	remember	recollect
crippled	disabled	rich	wealthy
disaster	calamity	sorrow	grief
edge	margin	start	commence
enemy	opponent	stick	adhere
freedom	liberty	stop	prohibit
friend	ally	story	narrative
give	contribute	understand	comprehend
happen	occur	weariness	fatigue

Synonyms of 'said'	Synonyms of 'good'	Synonyms of 'nice'	Synonyms of 'big'
stated	splendid	charming	huge
replied	delightful	beautiful	vast
shouted	fine	lovely	gigantic
announced	agreeable	attractive	extensive
asked	excellent	dainty	enormous
cried	noble	delicious	large
moaned	correct	pleasant	spacious
requested	useful	tasty	immense
spoke	valuable	graceful	mammoth
remarked	worthy	appealing	bulky
declared	great	enjoyable	massive
joked	beneficial	kind	burly
screamed			
grumbled			
confided			
admitted			
invited			
roared			
questioned			
whispered			
murmured			
exclaimed			
agreed			
interjected			

Antonyms

An antonym is a word that has the opposite meaning to another word.

hot → cold; happy → sad; quick → slow

Word	Antonym		Word	Antonym
accurate	inaccurate		essential	non-essential
amateur	professional		fact	fiction
agree	disagree		conscious	unconscious
energetic	lazy		innocent	guilty
behave	misbehave		legible	illegible
capture	release		conclusion	beginning
centralise	decentralise		mortal	immortal
expansion	contraction		majority	minority

English

Word	Antonym		Word	Antonym
regular	irregular		encourage	discourage
often	seldom		transparent	opaque
interior	exterior		maximum	minimum
positive	negative		trivial	important
ascend	descend		immigrant	emigrant
strengthen	weaken		vague	definite
import	export		careless	careful
temporary	permanent		voluntary	compulsory

Similes

A simile compares one thing with another and usually begins with the words 'as' or 'like'.

> Without his spectacles, Mr Johnson was <u>as blind as a bat</u>.
> The girl ran <u>like a deer</u>.

Some common similes are:

as blind as a bat	as greedy as a pig	as graceful as a swan
as flat as a pancake	as steady as a rock	as fresh as a daisy
as slippery as an eel	as quiet as a mouse	as slow as a snail
as cool as a cucumber	as quick as lightning	as safe as a bank
as cunning as a fox	as wise as an owl	as stubborn as a mule
as thin as a rake	as pretty as a picture	as light as a feather
as strong as an ox	as proud as a peacock	as white as a ghost
as clear as crystal	as fit as a fiddle	as cold as ice
as playful as a puppy	as busy as a bee	as dead as a doornail

Metaphors

A metaphor states that one thing is another. It does not include the words 'as' or 'like'.

> My friend Ben <u>is a sly fox</u>.

Occupations

The work people do is referred to as their occupation. People with some occupations have interesting names.

architect	designs plans for buildings
astrologer	claims to be able to tell the future by the stars
astronomer	studies the science of stars and the universe
auctioneer	sells things at an auction
aviator	flies planes
barrister	presents cases in a court of law
biographer	writes the story of someone's life
biologist	studies living things
florist	arranges and sells flowers
geologist	studies rocks and the surface of Earth
glazier	fits windows with glass
optician	makes optical instruments such as glasses
optometrist	tests eyesight
ornithologist	studies birds
psychologist	studies human behaviour
veterinarian	treats animal injuries and illnesses
zoologist	studies animals

Masculine and Feminine Words

Living things are usually classed as male or female. Words that describe these living things are said to be masculine or feminine gender. (The word 'gender' comes from a Latin word meaning 'what kind'.)

Masculine	Feminine	Masculine	Feminine
husband	wife	grandfather	grandmother
brother	sister	bridegroom	bride
nephew	niece	duke	duchess
uncle	aunt	father	mother
grandson	granddaughter	prince	princess
king	queen	boy	girl
drake	duck	gander	goose

English

Masculine	Feminine	Masculine	Feminine
ram	ewe	colt	filly
boar	sow	peacock	peahen
stallion	mare	bull	cow
buck	doe	fox	vixen

Locations

abbatoir   where livestock is killed for consumption

aviary   where birds are kept

crèche   where babies and small children are cared for

foundry   a metalworks plant

galley   the kitchen on a boat

gallery   where art is displayed

laboratory   where scientific research is carried out

monastery   where monks live

pharmacy   where medicines are dispensed

quarry   where rock is mined

Literature

There are many types of literature, including fiction, plays, short stories, poetry and non-fiction. When we read different types of literature, we may need to analyse the text to identify the plot, character, setting and text features. To fully understand the meaning of a text, we need to think about it, question it, look at different points of view, evaluate its relevance, and look deeper to find the author's motivation and message.

Character study:

A Venn diagram is useful to compare two characters. For example, this Venn diagram compares the different qualities of two characters in *Tomorrow When the War Began* by John Marsden.

Homer
problem
slob
macho
wild
crazy
immature
brave
leader

caring
considerate
thinker
listener
supportive

Lee
loving
introvert
intelligent
obsessive
dependable
mature
aggressive

Five Ws chart:

A 'Five Ws' chart can give a concise snapshot of the main plot of a text, such as this example from *The Forests of Silence* by Emily Rodda.

What happened?	The magic belt with seven gems has been stolen, dismantled and hidden. It needs to be found to protect the land and its king. Jared, Anna, Leif and Barda must find the topaz gem for the belt.
Who was there?	King Endon, his advisor Prandine, his friend Jared, Jared's son Leif, Jared's companion Barda, the Shadow Lord
Why did it happen?	Jared was suspicious about Prandine. When he tried to show King Endon information about the belt, Prandine accused him of trying to murder King Endon, so he fled.
When did it happen?	A long time ago
Where did it happen?	The land of Deltora

Story map:

A story map gives an overall picture of how the story starts, develops and arrives at its resolution.

Where	The land of Deltora
When	A long time ago
Major characters	Jared, Leif, Barda, Jasmine
Minor characters	Prandine, the Knight, Anna, Sharn, King Endon
Plot/problem	The magic belt with seven gems has been stolen, dismantled and hidden. It needs to be found to protect the land and its king. Jared, Anna, Leif and Barda must find the topaz gem for the belt.
Complication 1	King Endon and his wife swap places with Jared and Anna to hide.
Complication 2	Leif and Barda are in a deadly struggle with Gorl and the Lillies of Life.
Resolution/outcome	Jasmine saves Leif, who saves Barda. The three restore the topaz gem to the belt.

PMI table:

A PMI table can be helpful when creating a critical review of all parts of the text. It can be used to record pluses, minuses and interesting points about the text. It can also be used to discuss the plot, the setting, the characters, complications, writing style and so on.

Plus	Minus	Interesting

Literacy

Literacy broadens our understanding of the various uses of written, oral and digital text. It is important to recognise that text types differ depending on their purpose, their context, the writer's intention, the audience, the subject matter and the medium used.

Writing

Writing is one way that we can express our thoughts and feelings. We can use our imagination to create fictional stories about our favourite characters. In non-fiction writing, we can describe a science experiment, a trip to the beach or present information about our favourite animal.

Different kinds of writing, or 'genres', include stories, poems, reports, book reviews, advertisements, recipes, newspaper articles, newsletters, riddles, jokes, descriptions, poems, biographies, interviews, comic strips, procedures, letters, emails, diaries, journals, invitations, text messages, scripts, posters, blogs, greeting cards, captions and labels.

There are five stages in the writing process:

Planning
What is the purpose of your writing?
What are you going to write about?
Who will be your audience?
What form of writing, genre or text type will you use?

Drafting
Write your ideas, using the correct structure and language features of the text type you choose.
Refer to your planning notes.

Revising
Get some feedback.
Make changes, reorganise your ideas, rewrite and delete.
Read aloud to find mistakes.

Editing
Proofread and correct your spelling, grammar and punctuation.

Publishing
What is the best way to produce this piece of writing for your audience?

Text Types

Text Type	Purpose	Structure	Features	Forms
Recount	To retell and evaluate an event or experience	• Title • Orientation: who, when, what, where, why • Sequence of events: chronological order; paragraphs with topic sentences, supporting information, descriptive details; personal comment and evaluation	• First person narrative • Past-tense verbs • Time and sequence words • Adjective and adverbs • Reported speech	• Diary • Letter • Email • Journal • Blog • Magazine or newspaper article
Description	To describe the characteristics of a person, place or thing	• Title • Introduction: who, when, what, where, why • Characteristics: details about the subject; paragraphs with topic sentences, supporting information, descriptive details; personal comment and evaluation	• Present-tense verbs • Adjective and adverbs • Figurative language • Technical language	• Factual or fictional character description • Observation • Magazine or newspaper article • Oral presentation • Brochure or advertisement • Guidebook

English

Text Type	Purpose	Structure	Features	Forms
Narrative	To entertain or instruct by telling a series of events with a problem and solution	• Title • Orientation: who, where, when • Complication: with one or more problems • Sequence of events: paragraphs with topic sentences • Resolution: explains how the problem is solved; a moral or message	• Past-tense verbs • Time and sequence words • Adjective and adverbs • Direct speech • Figurative language	• Novel • Short story • Myth or legend • Biography • Play • Poem • Script • Song
Procedure	To provide instructions	• Title • Goal: what is going to be achieved, how to . . . • Materials: dot points, headings • Steps: sequence of events, headings, numerals, visual aids • Conclusion: summary	• Present-tense verbs • Adjectives and adverbs • Technical language • Commands	• Recipe • Game instructions • Instruction manual • Directions • Timetable • Experiment
Exposition (Persuasive)	To argue one side of an issue or convince others of a stated opinion or belief	• Title • Statement of belief: the writer's point of view • Arguments: paragraphs in order of importance with supporting evidence • Conclusion: reinforce statement of belief, offer solution or action	• Present-tense verbs • Time and sequence words • Connecting words • Reported speech • Persuasive language • Facts • Emotive language	• Letter • Speech • Lecture • Newspaper or magazine article • Advertisement • Letter to the editor • Editorial • Email • Essay

English

Text Type	Purpose	Structure	Features	Forms
Information Report	To present information that classifies living or non-living things	• Title • General statement: classify the subject • Description: paragraphs with topic sentences and supporting information • Evaluation: summary statement	• Present-tense verbs • Adjectives and adverbs • Technical language	• Reports • Newspaper report • Reference text • Brochure • Documentary • Manual • Research paper
Explanation	To explain how or why something happens	• Title • Identifying statement: what is to be explained • Opening paragraph: background information • Series of events: cause and effect, paragraphs with topic sentences and supporting information (how and why) • Summary statement	• Present-tense verbs • Adjectives and adverbs • Conjunctions • Connecting words • Technical language	• Oral presentation • Interview • Brochure • Newspaper or magazine article • Flow chart • Essay
Discussion	To examine all sides of an issue	• Title • Opening statement: background information • Arguments for: paragraphs in order of importance with supporting evidence • Arguments against: paragraphs in order of importance with supporting evidence • Conclusion: summary of the issue	• Present-tense verbs • Time and sequence words • Conjunctions • Connecting words • Reported speech • Persuasive language • Facts	• Speech • Debate • Newspaper or magazine article • Letter to the editor • Editorial • Lecture

English

Text Type	Purpose	Structure	Features	Forms
Response	To express an opinion about a text, object or event	• Title • Opening paragraph: context, background information • Description: paragraphs with topic sentences and supporting information about different aspects of the subject	• Present- or past-tense verbs • Adjectives and adverbs • Time and sequence words • Reported speech • Persuasive language • Figurative language	• Personal response • Review • Newspaper or magazine article • Journal
Poetry	Personal expression	• Many structures: acrostic, ballad, chant, cinquain, free verse, haiku, limerick, narrative, quatrain, rhyme	• Figurative language • Emotive language • Rhyme and rhythm	• Written • Spoken

Mathematics

The *Australian Curriculum: Mathematics* is organised around three content strands:

- **Number and Algebra**
- **Measurement and Geometry**
- **Statistics and Probability**

Students need to have proficiency in understanding, fluency, problem-solving and reasoning ability across all three content strands.

Signs and Symbols

$+$	**addition:** 'add', 'plus' or 'find the sum of'	$8 + 3 = 11$
$-$	**subtraction:** 'subtract', 'minus' or 'find the difference between'	$11 - 8 = 3$
$\times$	**multiplication:** 'multiply', 'times' or 'find the product of'	$8 \times 3 = 24$
$\div$	**division:** 'divide' or 'find the quotient of'	$24 \div 8 = 3$
$=$	**equal:** 'equals', 'is equal to'	$11 = 8 + 3$
$\neq$	**not equal:** 'is not equal to'	$12 \neq 8 + 3$
$\simeq$ or $\approx$	**approximately equal:** 'is approximately equal to'	$9.99 \approx 10$
$>$	**is greater than:** 'more than'	$12 > 8 + 3$
$<$	**is less than:** 'less than'	$8 + 3 < 12$
$\sqrt{}\ \sqrt[2]{}$	**square root:** 'the square root of'	$\sqrt{16} = 4$
$\sqrt[3]{}$	**cube root:** 'the cube root of'	$\sqrt[3]{8} = 2$
$\%$	**per cent:** 'per cent of' or 'per hundred'	$20\% = \dfrac{20}{100} = \dfrac{1}{5}$
$:$	**ratio:** 'is to'	$1{:}5 = \dfrac{1}{5}$
$\therefore$	**therefore**	
$@$	**at:** 5 cakes @ 20c each cost $1	
$\overline{AB}$	**line segment** or **interval:** AB	
$\overrightarrow{AB}$	**ray:** AB	
$\triangle$	**triangle:** $\triangle ABC$	
$\llcorner$	**angle:** $\angle XYZ$	
$^\circ$	**degrees:** 360°	
$\llcorner$	**right angle:** 90°	
$\perp$	**perpendicular:** 'at right angles to'	
$\parallel$	**parallel**	
π	**Pi:** approximately 3.14: for estimations, use 3	

Number and Algebra

Even Numbers

An even number ends with 2, 4, 6, 8 or 0 and can be divided evenly by 2, for example: 12.

Odd Numbers

An odd number ends with 1, 3, 5, 7 or 9 and can't be divided evenly by 2, for example: 13.

Prime Numbers

A prime number has no factors other than itself and 1. The prime numbers less than 30 are 2, 3, 5, 7, 11, 13, 17, 19, 23 and 29.

Composite Numbers

A composite number has other factors as well as itself and 1, for example: 12.

$$12 = 1 \times 12, 2 \times 6, 3 \times 4: \text{the factors of 12 are 1, 2, 3, 4, 6 and 12}$$

1 is neither a prime number nor a composite number.

Square Numbers

A square number has two factors of the same value, for example: 64.

$$64 = 8 \times 8$$

The square numbers to 100 are 1, 4, 9, 16, 25, 36, 49, 64, 81 and 100.

A square number can be shown by a square array:

1   4   9   16   and so on

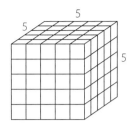

Cube Numbers

A cube number has three factors of the same value, for example: 125.

$$125 = 5 \times 5 \times 5$$

Triangular Numbers

A triangular number can be shown in a triangular pattern. The first triangular number is shown by a single dot, the second is shown by adding two more dots, the third by adding three more dots and so on:

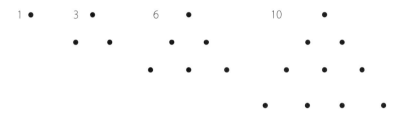

The triangular numbers to 100 are 1, 3, 6, 10, 15, 21, 28, 36, 45, 55, 66, 78 and 91. Any two successive triangular numbers added together form a square number.

$$28 + 36 = 64$$

Rectangular Numbers

A rectangular number can be shown by an array in the shape of a rectangle, for example: 24.

Factors

Factors are two numbers multiplied together to make another number, for example: 3 and 7 are factors of 21.

$$3 \times 7 = 21$$

Prime Factors

The prime factors of a number are the prime numbers that make up the product, for example: 2, 3 and 7 are the prime factors of 42. One way of finding the prime factors of a number is by using a factor tree:

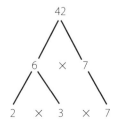

Mathematics

Common Factors

When two or more numbers have factors that are the same, these are called common factors, for example: 1, 2 and 4 are common factors of 24 and 20.

The factors of 24 are ①, ②, 3, ④, 6, 8, 12 and 24.
The factors of 20 are ①, ②, ④, 5, 10 and 20.

Highest Common Factor (HCF)

The highest common factor of two or more numbers is the common factor that has the greatest value, for example: the highest common factor of 30, 18 and 42 is 6.

The factors of 30 are ①, ②, ③, 5, ⑥, 10, 15 and 30.
The factors of 18 are ①, ②, ③, ⑥, 9 and 18.
The factors of 42 are ①, ②, ③, ⑥, 7, 14, 21 and 42.
The common factors of 30, 18 and 42 are 1, 2, 3 and 6.
The highest common factor is 6.

Multiples

Any product formed by multiplying two numbers together is a multiple of those numbers, for example: 36 is a multiple of both 4 and 9.

$$4 \times 9 = 36$$

Common Multiples

When two or more numbers have multiples that are same, these are called common multiples, for example: 18 and 36 are common multiples of 9 and 6.

Multiples of 9 (to 50) are 9, ⑱, 27, ㉟ and 45.
Multiples of 6 (to 50) are 6, 12, ⑱, 24, 30, ㉟, 42 and 48.

Lowest Common Multiple (LCM)

The lowest common multiple of two or more numbers is the common multiple that has the least value, for example: the lowest common multiple of 4 and 6 is 12.

Multiples of 4 (to 40) are 4, 8, ⑫, 16, 20, ㉔, 28, 32, ㊱ and 40.
Multiples of 6 (to 40) are 6, ⑫, 18, ㉔, 30 and ㊱.
The common multiples of 4 and 6 are 12, 24 and 36.
The lowest common factor is 12.

Product

When two numbers are multiplied together, the number that they form is called the product, for example: 5 multiplied by 6 gives a product of 30.

$$5 \times 6 = 30$$

Quotient

When a number is divided by another number, the result is called the quotient, for example: 48 divided by 4 gives a quotient of 12.

$$48 \div 4 = 12$$

Dividend

When a number is divided by another number, the number that is divided is called the dividend, for example: the dividend of 48 can be divided by 4 to give 12.

$$48 \div 4 = 12$$

Divisor

When a number is divided by another number, the number that it is divided by is called the divisor, for example: 48 can be divided by the divisor 4 to give 12.

$$48 \div 4 = 12$$

Exponents

An exponent (also called an index) is a number placed at the upper right of a number to show how many times that number is to be multiplied by itself, for example: in 4^2, 4 is the base number and the 2 is the exponent (or index).

$$4^2 = 4 \times 4 = 16$$
$$6^3 = 6 \times 6 \times 6 = 216$$

We can describe 4^2 as 'four squared' or 'four raised to the second power'.

We can describe 6^3 as 'six cubed' or 'six raised to the third power'.

Powers of Ten

Multiples of ten can be written in this form:

$$100 = 10 \times 10 = 10^2$$
$$1000 = 10 \times 10 \times 10 = 10^3$$
$$10\,000 = 10 \times 10 \times 10 \times 10 = 10^4$$
$$100\,000 = 10 \times 10 \times 10 \times 10 \times 10 = 10^5$$
$$1000\,000 = 10 \times 10 \times 10 \times 10 \times 10 \times 10 = 10^6$$

Square Root

The square root is the original number that was multiplied by itself to give a square number.

The square root of 49 is 7 because $7 \times 7 = 49$.

$$\sqrt{49} = 7$$

Cube Root

The cube root is the original number that was multiplied by itself three times to give a cube number.

$$\text{The cube root of 125 is 5 because } 5 \times 5 \times 5 = 125.$$
$$\sqrt[3]{125} = 5$$

Divisibility Rules

A number is divisible by 2 if it is an even number, for example: 10, 12, 14, 16, 18 . . . are divisible by 2.

A number is divisible by 3 if the sum of the digits is divisible by 3.

$$432: \text{sum of digits} = 9$$

A number is divisible by 4 if the number formed by the last two digits is divisible by 4.

$$728: 28 \div 4 = 7$$

A number is divisible by 5 if the last digit is 0 or 5, for example: 25, 30, 35, 40 . . . are divisible by 5.

A number is divisible by 6 if the sum of its digits is divisible by 3 and it is an even number.

$$822: \text{sum of digits} = 12, \text{even number}$$

There is no easy way to know if a number is divisible by 7.

A number is divisible by 8 if the number formed by the last three digits is divisible by 8.

$$79\,512: 512 \div 8 = 64$$

A number is divisible by 10 if the last digit is 0, for example: 10, 20, 30, 40 . . . are divisible by 10.

Roman Numerals

Hindu-Arabic numerals are the most common symbols used to represent numbers today. However, in Europe, the Roman numeral system was the most popular form of writing numbers until the Hindu-Arabic system became widely used in the sixteenth century. Today, Roman numerals can still be seen on some clock faces and are sometimes used to record dates (for example, at the end of a film to show when it was made, or on a public building to show when it was constructed or opened).

The Roman numeral system has no zero and all numerals are written using seven basic symbols: I (1), V (5), X (10), L (50), C (100), D (500), M (1000).

$$8 = \text{VIII} \qquad 106 = \text{CVI} \qquad 1989 = \text{MCMLXXXIX} \qquad 2041 = \text{MMXLI}$$

$|x| = 1$

Hindu-Arabic Numeral	Roman Numeral	Hindu-Arabic Numeral	Roman Numeral
1	I	60	LX
2	II	70	LXX
3	III	80	LXXX
4	IV	90	XC
5	V	100	C
6	VI	200	CC
7	VII	300	CCC
8	VIII	400	CD
9	IX	500	D
10	X	600	DC
20	XX	700	DCC
30	XXX	800	DCCC
40	XL	900	CM
50	L	1000	M

Ordinal Numbers

When objects are placed in a linear sequence, we use ordinal numbers to describe their position, for example: if ten children lined up to buy an ice-cream cone, the child at the front of the line would be first, the next child in the line would be second, and so on until the last child in line, who would be tenth. The ordinal numbers are first (1st), second (2nd), third (3rd), fourth (4th), fifth (5th), sixth (6th), seventh (7th), eighth (8th), ninth (9th), tenth (10th), eleventh (11th), twelfth (12th), thirteenth (13th), fourteenth (14th), fifteenth (15th), sixteenth (16th), seventeenth (17th), eighteenth (18th), nineteenth (19th), twentieth (20th), twenty-first (21st), twenty-second (22nd), twenty-third (23rd) . . .

Fractions

A fraction is a part of a whole that is divided into a number of equal parts or shares.

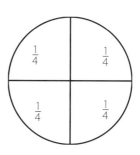

Common Fractions

A common fraction consists of two numbers separated by a line. The number above the line is called the numerator, and the number below the line is called the denominator. The line separating them is called the vinculum.

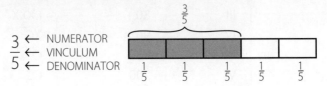

$$\frac{3}{5} \leftarrow \text{NUMERATOR}$$
$$\quad \leftarrow \text{VINCULUM}$$
$$\quad \leftarrow \text{DENOMINATOR}$$

The numerator shows the number of equal parts that make up the fraction.

The denominator shows the number of equal parts in the whole.

The fraction $\frac{3}{5}$ represents 3 out of 5 equal parts of the whole.

One whole equals two halves, three thirds, four quarters, etc.

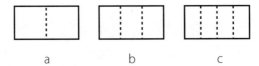

a   b   c

Proper Fractions

A proper fraction has a numerator that is smaller than the denominator (that is, its value is less than one).

$$\frac{7}{10}$$

Improper Fractions

An improper fraction has a numerator that is equal to or greater then the denominator (that is, its value is equal to or greater than one).

$$\frac{4}{3}$$

An improper fraction can also be written as a mixed number.

$$1\frac{1}{3}$$

Mixed Numbers

A mixed number is made up of a whole number and a fraction.

$$1\frac{1}{3}$$

A mixed number can also be written as an improper fraction.

$$\frac{4}{3}$$

Equivalent Fractions

Equivalent fractions are different fractions that represent the same part of the whole.

$\frac{3}{4}$ is equivalent to $\frac{6}{8}$

The value of a fraction stays the same when the numerator and the denominator are *both* multiplied by the same number.

$$\frac{3}{4} = \frac{3 \times 2}{4 \times 2} = \frac{6}{8} \qquad \frac{2}{3} = \frac{2 \times 12}{3 \times 12} = \frac{24}{36}$$

The value of a fraction stays the same when the numerator and denominator are *both* divided by the same number – that is, by a common factor – to find their lowest terms.

$$\frac{6}{8} = \frac{6 \div 2}{8 \div 2} = \frac{3}{4} \qquad \frac{24}{36} = \frac{24 \div 12}{36 \div 12} = \frac{2}{3}$$

Decimal Fractions and Percentages

Our money system is a decimal fraction system that uses one dollar as a whole and cents as hundredths of a dollar, for example: \$6.37 can be thought of as $6\frac{37}{100}$.

To write a common fraction as a decimal fraction, the denominator of the common fraction must first be in the form of a multiple of 10.

$$7\frac{4}{5} = 7\frac{8}{10} = 7.8 \qquad 13\frac{1}{4} = 13\frac{25}{100} = 13.25$$

The term 'percentage' comes from the Latin words *per centum* meaning 'out of one hundred'. We often use percentages in everyday life; for example, shops often display signs saying '20% OFF' or '10% DISCOUNT'. Percentages are fractions with a denominator of 100, for example: five per cent means five parts out of 100 equal parts.

$$5\% = \frac{5}{100} = \frac{1}{20} = 0.05$$

Percentage	Common Fraction	Decimal Fraction
1%	$\frac{1}{100}$	0.01
2%	$\frac{2}{100} = \frac{1}{50}$	0.02
5%	$\frac{5}{100} = \frac{1}{20}$	0.05
10%	$\frac{10}{100} = \frac{1}{10}$	0.1
20%	$\frac{20}{100} = \frac{1}{5}$	0.2
25%	$\frac{25}{100} = \frac{1}{4}$	0.25
30%	$\frac{30}{100} = \frac{3}{10}$	0.3
50%	$\frac{50}{100} = \frac{1}{2}$	0.5
75%	$\frac{75}{100} = \frac{3}{4}$	0.75
100%	$\frac{100}{100} = 1$	1

Mathematics

Recurring Decimals

The answer to a division sum usually has a limited number of decimal places. Sometimes though, the answer will never stop, as there is always a remainder. For example:

$$3 \overline{)8} \quad \overset{2.666...}{} \quad \text{or} \quad 2.\dot{6}$$

When 8 is divided by 3, the dot above the 6 shows that it is repeated forever. This is called a recurring decimal.

Measurement and Geometry

Measures of Time

60 seconds (s) = 1 minute (min)

60 minutes (min) = 1 hour (h)

24 hours (h) = 1 day

7 days   = 1 week

2 weeks = 1 fortnight

4 weeks = 1 month

52 weeks = 1 year

365 days = 1 year

366 days = 1 leap year

12 months = 1 year

10 years = 1 decade

100 years = 1 century

Days of the Week

Sunday, Monday, Tuesday, Wednesday, Thursday, Friday, Saturday

Months of the Year

January (31 days)

February (28 days or 29 days – leap year)

March (31 days)

April (30 days)

May (31 days)

June (30 days)

July (31 days)

August (31 days)

September (30 days)

October (31 days)

November (30 days)

December (31 days)

Leap Year

In a leap year, an extra day is added to the month of February to make 29 days.
A leap year usually occurs in every year that is evenly divisible by four (such as 1972).
The exceptions are the 'century' years (such as 1700, 1800 and 1900); they are only
leap years if they are divisible evenly by 400. Therefore, 1900 was not a leap year but
2000 was.

Terms of Time

am (ante meridiem, Latin for 'before noon') the time between midnight and midday

pm (post meridiem, Latin for 'after noon') the time between midday and midnight

analogue time the time on a traditional clock face
> eight forty-five
> a quarter to nine

digital time the time on a digital clock

> 8:45 am
> 8:45 pm

24-hour time the time used by the military, in timetables and in schedules, where 12 is added to the 'hour' part of pm times
> 0845
> 2045

Greenwich Mean Time time based on an imaginary line at 0° longitude at Greenwich Observatory in England. Times around the world are calculated from this meridian. There are three time zones in Australia:

Eastern Standard Time (10 hours ahead of Greenwich) is used in Queensland, New South Wales, Victoria and Tasmania

Central Standard Time (9 hours 30 minutes ahead of Greenwich) is used in South Australia and the Northern Territory

Western Standard Time (8 hours ahead of Greenwich) is used in Western Australia

International Date Line an imaginary line that marks where in the world each new calendar day begins. It follows the 180th meridian for most of its distance. If you cross the International Date Line going east, you go backwards a day. If you cross it going west, you go forwards a day.

The Gregorian Calendar the calendar we use, with 1 January as the first day of the year.

Years are numbered from the beginning of the 'Common Era', for example:
> The First Fleet arrived in Australia in 1788 CE.

Events before 1 CE are described as 'before the Common Era', for example:
> Indigenous people lived in Australia from up to 40 000 BCE.

Metric Measurements

Measures of Length

10 millimetres (mm) = 1 centimetre (cm)

100 centimetres (cm) = 1 metre (m)

1000 millimetres (mm) = 1 metre (m)

1000 metres (m) = 1 kilometre (km)

Measures of Mass

1000 milligrams (mg) = 1 gram (g)

1000 grams (g) =1 kilogram (kg)

1000 kilograms (kg) = 1 tonne (t)

Measures of Area

100 square millimetres (mm^2) = 1 square centimetre (cm^2)

10 000 square centimetres (cm^2) = 1 square metre (m^2)

10 000 square metres (m^2) = 1 hectare (ha)

100 hectares (ha) = 1 square kilometre (km^2)

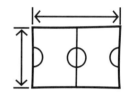

Measures of Capacity (Fluid)

1000 millilitres (mL) = 1 litre (L)

1000 litres (L) = 1 kilolitre (kL)

Measures of Volume

1000 cubic millimetres (mm^3) = 1 cubic centimetre (cm^3)

1 000 000 cubic centimetres (cm^3) = 1 cubic metre (m^3)

Measurements of Data

1024 bytes = 1 kilobyte

1024 kilobytes = 1 megabyte

1024 megabytes = 1 gigabyte

Temperature

Temperature is a measure of how hot or cold something is. It is measured using a thermometer. There are two common scales of temperature: Fahrenheit and Celsius. In Australia, we use the Celsius scale.

On the Celsius scale:

- the boiling point of water is 100°C
- the freezing point of water is 0°C
- the normal body temperature of a human is approximately 37°C

On the Fahrenheit scale:

- the boiling point of water is 212°F
- the freezing point of water is 32°F
- the normal body temperature of a human is approximately 94°F

Money Systems

Money is the currency that people agree to accept in exchange for the service they provide, the product they make or the work that they do. In the past, people used various forms of currency, such as shells or animals. Today, most countries use coins, paper money, credit and debit cards and bank cheques.

Each country has its own units of money; for example, Japan uses the yen and Australia uses the dollar. These basic units are broken down into smaller units of money; for example, the Australian dollar equals 100 cents.

Currencies around the World

Australia	Australian dollar	Mexico	peso
China	yuan	Canada	Canadian dollar
Germany, France, Italy	euro	Thailand	baht
Great Britain	pound sterling	Vietnam	dang
India	rupee	Sweden	krona
Japan	yen	South Africa	rand
New Zealand	New Zealand dollar	Papua New Guinea	kina
Switzerland	franc	Singapore	Singapore dollar
United States of America	US dollar	Indonesia	rupiah
Russia	ruble	Malaysia	ringgit
Cambodia	riel	Laos	kip

Lines and Angles

Point

A point is a position in space shown by a dot.

Line

A straight line is the shortest possible distance between two points. It can be extended in both directions without ending.

Line Segment

A line segment (or interval) is the part of a line between two given points.

Parallel Lines

Parallel lines are straight lines that are always the same distance apart and will never meet.

Horizontal Lines

A horizontal line is a straight line running parallel to the horizon.

Vertical line

A vertical line is a straight line running at right angles (90°) to the horizon.

Oblique line

An oblique line is one that lives between the horizontal and vertical positions.

Perpendicular Lines

Perpendicular lines run at right angles (90°) to each other.

AB is perpendicular to *CD*
XY is perpendicular to *PQ*

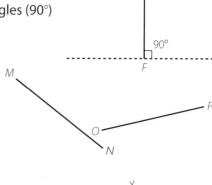

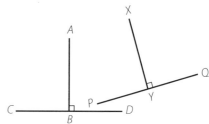

Ray

A ray is a line that has a fixed starting point (origin) but no end.

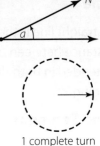

STARTING POINT (ORIGIN)

Angle

An angle is formed when two lines intersect or when a ray is rotated about its origin.

> The angle at *P* is formed when *PS* is rotated to *PN*.
>
> *P* is the vertex of this angle.
>
> The angle at *P* is written $\underline{\angle NPS}$ or *a*.

The size of an angle indicates the amount of rotation and is measured in degrees. One complete rotation (a revolution) is divided into 360 equal parts and each part is one degree (1°).

1 complete turn (1 revolution) = 360°

Right Angle

A right angle measures 90° (a quarter of a complete turn).

$$\underline{\angle JKL} = b = 90°$$

Acute Angle

An acute angle measures less than 90°.

$$\underline{\angle MPN} = c < 90°$$

Obtuse Angle

An obtuse angle measures more than 90° but less than 180°.

$$\underline{\angle RST} = 90° < d < 180°$$

Straight Angle

ABC is a straight line. The angle at B is a straight angle and measures 180° (half a complete rotation).

$$\underline{\angle ABC} = 180°$$

Reflex Angle

A reflex angle is greater than a straight angle (180°) but less than a complete revolution (360°). It is the other angle formed when an acute or an obtuse angle is drawn.

$$180° < a < 360°$$

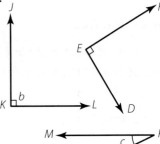

REFLEX ANGLE

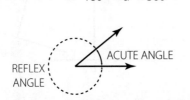

REFLEX ANGLE   ACUTE ANGLE

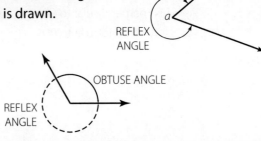

REFLEX ANGLE   OBTUSE ANGLE

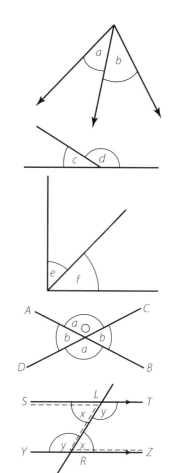

Adjacent Angles

Adjacent angles are two angles with a common ray.

Supplementary Angle

A supplementary angle is formed by two adjacent angles that have a sum of 180°.

Complementary Angle

A complementary angle is formed by two adjacent angles that have a sum of 90°.

Vertically Opposite Angles

When two straight lines intersect, the opposite angles are equal.

$$\underline{|AOC} = \underline{|DOB}$$
$$\underline{|AOD} = \underline{|COB}$$

Alternate Angles

When two parallel lines are intersected by a straight line, the alternate angles are equal.

$$\underline{|TLR} = \underline{|LRY}$$
$$\underline{|SLR} = \underline{|LRZ}$$

Two-dimensional Shapes

A two-dimensional (2D or 'plane') shape has length and width (breadth) but no depth. The perimeter of a 2D shape is the distance around the outside of it. The area is the space covered by that shape.

Polygon

A polygon is a 2D shape with any number of sides formed by straight lines.

POLYGON

Quadrilateral

A quadrilateral is any four-sided polygon.

QUADRILATERAL

Trapezoid

A trapezoid is a quadrilateral with one set of parallel sides of unequal length.

TRAPEZOID

Parallelogram

A parallelogram is a quadrilateral with two sets of parallel sides of equal length.

PARALLELOGRAM

Rhombus

A rhombus is a parallelogram with parallel opposite sides of equal length.

RHOMBUS

Pentagon

A pentagon is a polygon with five sides.

A regular pentagon has all sides of equal length and equal interior angles. Regular polygons include:

REGULAR
PENTAGON

HEXAGON − SIX SIDES

HEPTAGON − SEVEN SIDES

OCTAGON − EIGHT SIDES

NONAGON − NINE SIDES

DECAGON − TEN SIDES

Rectangle

A rectangle is a quadrilateral. Its opposite sides are parallel and of equal length so it is a kind of parallelogram. All its angles are right angles.

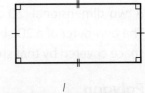

The rule for finding the perimeter of a rectangle is:

Perimeter = (Length + Width) × 2

$P = (l + w) \times 2$

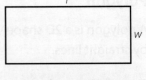

The rule for finding the area of a rectangle is:

Area = Length × Width

$A = l \times w$

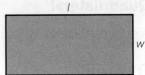

$1 \times 1 = 1$

Square

A square is a kind of rectangle. It is also a type of rhombus. It has four sides of equal length and all its angles are right angles.

The rule for finding the perimeter of a square is:

Perimeter = Side × 4

$P = s \times 4$

The rule for finding the area of a square is:

Area = Side × Side = Side²

$A = s^2$

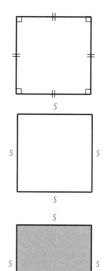

Triangle

A triangle is a three-sided polygon. The sum of the angles in any triangle is always 180°.

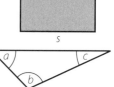

$a + b + c = 180°$

The rule for finding the perimeter of a triangle is:

Perimeter = Side + Side + Side ($P = s + s + s$)

(or $P = s \times 3$ for an equilateral triangle)

The rule for finding the area of a triangle is:

Area = Base × Height ÷ 2

$$A = \frac{b \times h}{2}$$

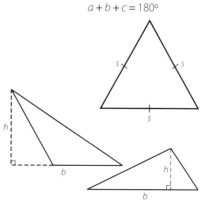

Equilateral Triangle

An equilateral triangle has all sides of equal length and all angles measure 60°.

$$AB = BC = CA$$

Isosceles Triangle

An isosceles triangle has two sides of equal length and the angles opposite these sides are equal.

$$MN = NO \qquad \underline{/NMO} = \underline{/NOM}$$

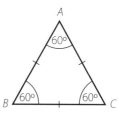

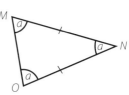

Scalene Triangle

A scalene triangle has three sides of different length and all angles are unequal.

Right-angled Triangle

A right-angled triangle has one right angle and two acute angles.

$$\underline{|PQR} = 90°$$

In any right-angled triangle, the square on the longest side opposite the right angle (the hypotenuse) equals the sum of the squares on the other two sides.

$$a^2 + b^2 = c^2$$

Acute-angled Triangle

An acute-angled triangle has all angles less than 90°.

Obtuse-angled Triangle

An obtuse-angled triangle has only one obtuse angle.

Circle

A circle is a closed curve. The centre of a circle is an equal distance from any point on the curve.

Circumference

The circumference is the curved line of the circle.

Chord

A chord is a straight line that cuts the circumference of the circle at two points.

Diameter

The diameter (d) is a special chord. It a straight line that passes through the centre of the circle and divides it into two equal parts.

$|x| = 1$

Radius

The radius (*r*) is a line from the centre of the circle to any point on the circumference. The length of the radius is half the length of the diameter of that circle.

$$r = d \div 2$$

$$d = 2 \times r$$

Pi

The Greek letter pi (written π) stands for the number of times the diameter of a circle will fit around the circumference of the circle.

π = Circumference ÷ Diameter

Pi is given an approximate value of 3.14. The rule for finding the circumference of a circle is:

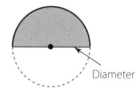

Diameter

Circumference = $\pi \times$ Diameter

$$= 2\,\pi r$$

The rule for finding the area of a circle is:

$$\text{Area} = \pi r^2$$

Semicircle

A semicircle is half a circle.

Quadrant

A quadrant is one quarter of a circle.

Arc

An arc is part of the circumference of a circle.

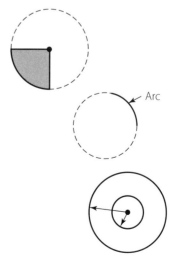

Arc

Concentric Circles

Concentric circles have the same centre point but radii of different lengths.

Three-dimensional Objects

A three-dimensional (3D or 'solid') object has length, width (breadth) and depth. A solid object may have flat or curved surfaces (faces). It has edges and its corners are called vertices. The volume of a 3D object is the space taken up by that shape.

Rectangular Prism

A rectangular prism has six faces. Each face is a rectangle and all its angles are right angles. Its opposite faces are equal and parallel.

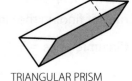

RECTANGULAR PRISM

Triangular Prism

In a triangular prism, the bases or ends are triangular and there are three side faces. Each of the side faces is a parallelogram.

TRIANGULAR PRISM

Cube

A cube has six square faces. All sides of a cube are of equal length and all its angles are 90°.

CUBE

Cylinder

A cylinder has two circular bases or ends and its face is a curved surface.

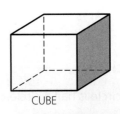

CYLINDER

Pyramid

A pyramid has a base that is square or triangular. The side faces are triangular and meet at a point called the vertex.

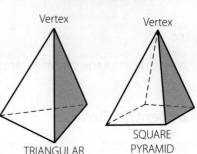

Vertex　　　　　Vertex

TRIANGULAR
PYRAMID

SQUARE
PYRAMID

Mathematics

$1 \times 1 = 1$

Cone

A cone has a circular base and a curved surface that comes to a point called the apex.

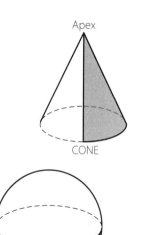

Sphere

A sphere is a curved ball or globe that has no corners or edges. Each point on the surface is the same distance from the centre.

Graphs

A graph is a chart that is used to show many types of data in a visual form. A graph always has a title and two labelled axes – the x axis along the bottom and the y axis along the left upright side. There are several kinds of graphs:

• a bar graph shows data with vertical or horizontal bars

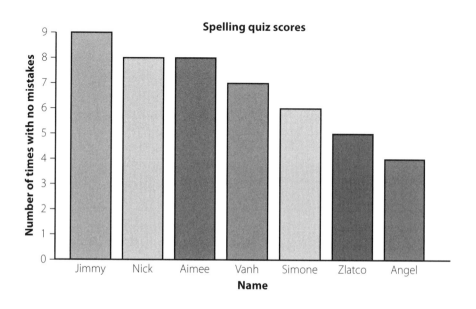

- a picture graph shows data with simple pictures

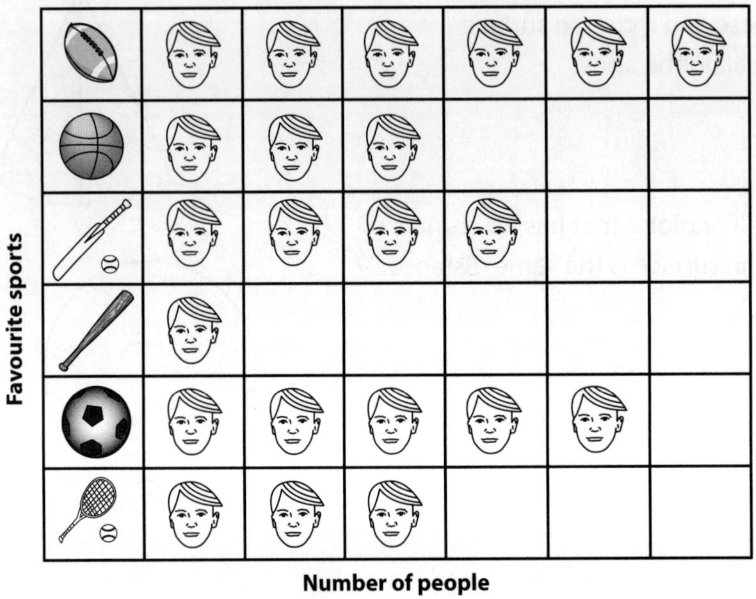

- A pie graph shows data as parts of a circle. To construct a pie graph, you must first construct a table of data with amounts in ascending order. Add up the total of the amounts and use this to turn each amount into a fraction.

Students' favourite shoes	Fraction	Value in degrees
Runners – 30	$\frac{30}{60}$	$\frac{30}{60} \times \frac{360}{1} = \frac{10800}{60} = 180$
School shoes – 12	$\frac{12}{60}$	$\frac{12}{60} \times \frac{360}{1} = \frac{4320}{60} = 72$
Boots – 6	$\frac{6}{60}$	$\frac{6}{60} \times \frac{360}{1} = \frac{2160}{60} = 36$
Slippers – 6	$\frac{6}{60}$	$\frac{6}{60} \times \frac{360}{1} = \frac{2160}{60} = 36$
Thongs – 3	$\frac{3}{60}$	$\frac{3}{60} \times \frac{360}{1} = \frac{1080}{60} = 18$
Sandals – 3	$\frac{3}{60}$	$\frac{3}{60} \times \frac{360}{1} = \frac{1080}{60} = 18$
Total – 60	$\frac{60}{60}$	360

Multiply each fraction by 360 to find its value in degrees (there are 360 degrees in a circle).

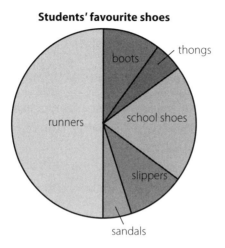

Students' favourite shoes

Use a compass to draw a circle. Draw a radius from the middle and use the degree values from your table to create segments for each amount. Give your graph a title and label each segment correctly.

Statistics and Probability

Tally Marks

Tally marks are an easy way of keeping track of numbers in groups of five. A vertical line is made for each of the first four numbers, than a diagonal line is made across the first four lines to show the fifth number.

Ratio

A ratio shows the relationship between two numbers. Ratios are used to show the scale on a map or the amount of ingredients needed in a recipe. For example, if you put two cups of flour into a mixture for every cup of sugar, the ratio of flour to sugar can be shown as 2:1; if you use a distance of one centimetre on a map to represent 10 kilometres in real life, the ratio of centimetres to kilometres can be shown as 1:10.

Probability

Probability is the measure of how likely an event or outcome is to happen. For example, if you toss a coin, there is a 'one in two' chance of tossing a head or tail (this can be shown as 1:2). If you spin a spinner that is divided into four equal parts with four different colours, there is a 'one in four' chance of it stopping on a particular colour (1:4).

Mean, Mode, Median and Range

Another word for the term 'mean' is 'average'. The mean or average is the middle point of a group of numbers. To calculate the mean, add all the numbers in the set then divide by the amount of numbers in the set.

> 7, 4, 11, 5, 13
> 40 is the sum of the numbers in the set
> 40 ÷ 5 = 8
> 8 is the mean (average)

The mode is the number that occurs most often in a set of numbers.

> 34, 26, 38, 41, 34, 37, 26, 34
> 34 occurs three times in the set
> 34 is the mode

The median is the middle number in a set where the numbers have been arranged in ascending order from smallest to biggest.

> 47, 35, 37, 32, 38, 39, 34, 35, 36
> 32, 34, 35, 35, 36, 37, 38, 39, 47 – the numbers arranged in ascending order
> the middle number is 36
> 36 is the median

If two numbers are left in the middle of a set, then the median is the average of those two numbers.

> 23, 39, 14, 27, 26, 33
> 14, 23, 26, 27, 33, 39 – the numbers arranged in ascending order
> the middle numbers are 26 and 27
> 53 is the sum of the two numbers
> 53 ÷ 2 = 26.5
> 26.5 is the median

The range is the difference between the biggest and smallest number in the same set.

> Tommy has 40 marbles, Jim has 22 marbles, Tim has 34 marbles, Jason has 28 marbles.
> The range = 40 marbles (biggest) minus 22 marbles (smallest)
> 40 – 22 = 18
> 18 is the range

Science

The *Australian Curriculum: Science* is organised around three connected strands:

- **Scientific Understanding**
- **Scientific Inquiry Skills**
- **Science as a Human Endeavour**

Learning about science begins at a very early age when young children are curious about the world around them. At all stages of our life, we frequently ask questions to try and gain an understanding about ourselves and the world around us, so we can function effectively in a scientifically and technically advanced society.

Process Skills

Observation

Observing is the most basic skill used in science. It includes any of the five senses – sight, touch, taste, hearing, smell.

Prediction

Predicting what might happen must be based on the result of an observation, otherwise it is only a guess. For example, weather forecasts are predictions about weather that are made by referring to records of similar weather patterns in the past.

Inference

Inferring is using what you have observed to create an explanation. Several inferences can sometimes be made from one observation, but inferences are not always correct. Further tests may be needed to confirm an inference or to show that it is incorrect.

> I observed that caramel tastes sweet. I inferred that caramel contains sugar.

Classification

Scientists often group together, or classify, things that have similar characteristics. Classification can make the study of a group of things more meaningful. For example, a botanist might classify plants according to the type or number of leaves they have.

A group of things can be classified in different ways according to what is being studied. For example, a botanist might classify the same plants in a different way if they are studying root structure instead of leaf growth.

Measurement

During their experiments, scientists often need to measure length, mass, volume, time and temperature. They need to use standard metric measurements so that the results of their experiments can be recognised by other scientists around the world.

Writing Reports

Scientists need to write the results of their experiments correctly in their reports.
A scientific report should include:

- a title

    The Greenhouse Effect

- the aim

    to show how the greenhouse effect works

- the hypothesis – what you think might happen

    the temperature in the plastic bag will rise

- equipment

    two thermometers
    a plastic bag

- the procedure

    1. Put a thermometer inside the plastic bag and seal it.
    2. Put the plastic bag outside in direct sunlight with another thermometer outside the bag.

- the results – data from observations

    graphs, diagrams, tables

Time	Thermometer in Bag	Single Thermometer
10 am	38 degrees	33 degrees
11 am	40 degrees	34 degrees
12 pm	43 degrees	34 degrees

- conclusion – summary and analysis, what and why, inference

History/Australian Studies

Facts about Australia

Australia is in the Southern Hemisphere. With an area of 7 692 024 square kilometres, it is the smallest, flattest and driest continent, but it is also the largest island and the sixth largest country in the world. Neighbouring countries include New Zealand, Indonesia and Papua New Guinea. The capital city of Australia is Canberra, in the Australian Capital Territory (ACT). The capital cities of the other states and territories are Melbourne (Victoria), Sydney (New South Wales [NSW]), Adelaide (South Australia [SA]), Brisbane (Queensland [QLD]), Perth (Western Australia [WA]), Hobart (Tasmania) and Darwin (Northern Territory [NT]).

Australia has a population of more than 22 million and it is one of the world's most urbanised countries, with about 70 per cent of the population living in the ten largest cities – mainly on the east coast. It has a culturally diverse society that includes indigenous people and immigrants from over 200 different countries.

The Australian economy is based on service industries, agriculture and mining resources. Australia is a major exporter of agricultural products such as wheat and wool, minerals such as iron ore and gold, and energy such as natural gas and coal.

The national anthem of Australia is 'Advance Australia Fair'. The Australian flag features the Southern Cross (representing Australia's geographic position in the Southern Hemisphere), the seven-pointed Commonwealth Star (representing the six states and the territories) and the Union Jack (the British flag – a reminder of the early European settlers).

The Australian coat of arms is made up of a shield that features the emblems of each of the six states. The Commonwealth Star appears above the shield and branches of wattle form the background. The shield is supported by a kangaroo and an emu.

Physical Features

Highest mountain: Mount Kosciusko (2228 m), NSW

Largest river system: Murray River (2375 km in length) and the Murray-Darling basin, Victoria, NSW and SA

Lowest point: Lake Eyre (approximately 15 m below sea level), SA

Largest desert: Great Victoria Desert (348 750 sq km), WA and SA

The Great Barrier Reef: the largest expanse of coral reefs in the world (over 2000 km long), QLD

Uluru: the largest monolith in the world (345 m high, an area of 3 sq km and 10 km around the base), NT

Fraser Island: the largest sand island in the world, QLD

Government in Australia

The Australian system of government is a democracy. Australia was declared a federation in 1901 and now has a federal government, six state governments and two self-governing territories. Australia has compulsory voting at the federal and state level.

Federal Government

The federal government is also referred to as the Commonwealth government. It is based in Canberra and deals with issues that affect Australia as a nation, including foreign affairs, defence, customs and immigration, taxation, social services, immigration, postal services, trade and commerce. In 1901, when the Commonwealth of Australia was proclaimed, a federal constitution was established to set out the powers of the federal government. If the federal government wants to alter the constitution, it has to hold a referendum where all Australian electors must vote 'yes' or 'no' to the proposed change. For the change to become part of the constitution, it must be agreed to by a majority of Australian voters and by a majority of voters in at least four of the six states. Over the years, Australian voters have approved only eight changes, from 42 proposals, to the constitution.

The Governor-General

This is the representative of the King or Queen in Australia. The Governor-General's main residence, Yarralumla, is in Canberra. The Governor-General is nominated by the federal government and approved by the King or Queen of the Commonwealth.

The Prime Minister

This is the leader of the party (or coalition of parties) with the most members in the Federal Parliament. The prime minister is the leader of the federal government.

The Leader of the Opposition

This is the leader of the party (or coalition of parties) with the most members in opposition.

The House of Representatives

This is the lower house of the Federal Parliament. The 147 members are called Members of Parliament (MPs). They are elected by the people to represent different areas, or electorates. The Prime Minister and the Leader of the Opposition are members of the House of Representatives.

The Senate

This is the upper house of the Federal Parliament. The members are called senators. Each state has 12 senators who are elected by the people. The Northern Territory and the Australian Capital Territory have two senators each.

State Government

The state governments are based in the capital city of each state and deal with issues that affect the states, including railways, police, education, roads and traffic, industry, housing, ports and hospitals. The two territories (ACT and NT) have their own governments but their powers are less than the other state governments.

The Governor

This is the representative of the King or Queen in each state of Australia. The Governor is nominated by the state government and approved by the King or Queen of the Commonwealth.

The Premier

This is the leader of the party (or coalition of parties) with the most members in the State Parliament. The Premier is the leader of the state government.

The Leader of the Opposition

This is the leader of the party (or coalition of parties) with the most members in opposition.

State Parliament

The organisation of State Parliaments can vary from state to state. For example, the lower house of the State Parliament of Victoria, NSW and WA is called the Legislative

Assembly. In Tasmania and SA it is called the House of Assembly. Queensland only has one house in its State Parliament.

Local Government

There are more than 850 local governments based in cities, towns and country areas across the states. They deal with local issues such as traffic, parks, libraries, street lighting and waste collection. Local governments are called councils. The leader of the council is called the Lord Mayor in a capital city, the Mayor in smaller cities and towns, or the Shire President or Chairperson in regional districts. The members of local councils are called councillors.

Government Terminology

Act of Parliament

This is a bill that has been passed by the Federal or State Parliament, signed by the Governor-General (Federal Parliament) or the Governor (State Parliament), and then proclaimed as a law.

Amendment

This is an alteration made to a bill that is being debated by Federal or State Parliament.

Ballot paper

This is the paper that shows the names of candidates for a local, state or federal election. Voters mark their preferences to vote for their preferred candidate.

Bill

This is a proposal put before State or Federal Parliament which, if passed and then signed by the Governor-General (Federal Parliament) or Governor (State Parliament), will become law.

Budget

This is the local, state or federal government's annual financial statement of income and expenditure. It is presented to State or Federal Parliament by the Treasurer.

By-election

When a Member of Parliament dies, resigns or is expelled from the Parliament during the term of a government, an election is held in that member's electorate to fill the vacancy. This is called a by-election.

Cabinet

This is the committee of government ministers that decides policy and makes day-to-day decisions of government.

Coalition

This is an alliance between two or more political parties. They work together to form the government or opposition in the State or Federal Parliament.

Democracy

This is a system of government where the people elect their representatives.

Electorate

This is the area in which people vote to elect a representative in their state or federal government.

Independent

This is a candidate, Member of Parliament or Senator who is not a member of a political party.

Minister

This is a member of the government who is appointed to administer a particular area of responsibility, such as the Minister for Education or the Minister for Health and Community Services.

Portfolio

This is an area of government responsibility, such as education, health or finance, that is allocated to a particular minister.

Quorum

This is the minimum number of members of parliament that needs to be present in the House of Representatives in the Federal Parliament (or equivalent house in a State Parliament) before government business may be discussed.

Speaker

This is the title given to a Member of Parliament who is appointed by their colleagues to act as the chairperson when the House of Representatives in the Federal Parliament (or equivalent house in a State Parliament) is in session. In the Senate in the Federal Parliament, this person is called the President of the Senate.

Treasurer

This is the minister responsible for the government's budget and finances.

Ward

This is the name given to the electoral divisions within an area of local government in towns and cities.

Important Dates in Australian History

For more than 40 000 years before Europeans settled in Australia, Aboriginal and Torres Strait Islander people inhabited most areas of the continent. There were hundreds of separate languages, lifestyles and cultural traditions that varied from region to region. Indigenous people had complex social systems and traditions that were based on a deep spiritual and cultural connection with the land and the environment.

1606	The Dutch explorer Willem Janszoon charted the west coast of Cape York Peninsula in Queensland. This was the first recorded European contact with Australia.
1688	William Dampier became the first British explorer to land on the Australian coast.
1770	Captain James Cook claimed the east coast of Australia for England and named it New South Wales.
1788	Captain Arthur Phillip arrived with the First Fleet and established the first European settlement, a penal colony, at Port Jackson (Sydney Harbour) on 26 January. This date is now known as Australia Day.
1790	The Second Fleet arrived.
1801–03	Matthew Flinders circumnavigated Australia in the *Investigator*, exploring and charting the coastline and giving an accurate picture of its size and shape.
1803	Governor King sent Lieutenant John Bowen with soldiers and convicts to Van Diemen's Land (Tasmania) to establish a settlement on the Derwent River at Risdon Cove. The next year, another party under Lieutenant-Colonel David Collins settled at the present site of Hobart.
	Australia's first newspaper, the *Sydney Gazette*, was published.
1813	The first route from the coastal plains to the inland was opened up when Blaxland, Lawson and Wentworth crossed the Blue Mountains west of Sydney.
1817	Australia's first bank, the Bank of New South Wales, was established.
1824	The first settlement in Queensland, a penal colony, was established near Redcliffe on Moreton Bay. Early the following year, the settlement was moved to the present site of Brisbane.
1825	Van Diemen's Land was declared a separate colony from New South Wales, with Colonel George Arthur as Lieutenant-Governor.
1829	Captain James Stirling was appointed Lieutenant-Governor of the new Swan River colony at Perth in Western Australia.

1829–30	Charles Sturt travelled down the Murrumbidgee River and then along the Murray River to its mouth, solving the mystery of where the great inland river systems ended.
1835	John Batman – and, a few months later, John Fawkner – chose land near the mouth of the Yarra River as the site for the settlement that was later named Melbourne.
1836	The first colonists reached South Australia and Colonel William Light surveyed Adelaide as the site for the settlement. Captain John Hindmarsh was the first governor of the colony.
1851	The Port Phillip District became a separate colony of Victoria, with Charles La Trobe as lieutenant-governor.
	Edward Hargraves discovered gold near Bathurst in NSW and the Victorian gold rush began with the discovery of gold near Ballarat.
1852	The last transportation of convicts from Britain to eastern Australia took place.
1854	The battle of the Eureka Stockade was fought between gold-diggers and government forces at Ballarat in Victoria.
1859	The Moreton Bay District became a separate colony of Queensland, with Sir George Bowen as its first governor.
1860–61	Burke and Wills were the first Europeans to cross Australia from south to north. Neither survived the return journey.
1868	The last transportation of convicts from Britain to Western Australia took place.
1869	The children of some Aboriginal and Torres Strait Islanders were removed from their families by government authorities, a process that would continue into the next century. These children became known as 'the Stolen Generation'.
1872	The construction of the Overland Telegraph Line from Port Augusta to Darwin was completed.
1873	Uluru was first sighted by Europeans, who called it Ayers Rock.
1880	The bushranger Ned Kelly was hanged at the Old Melbourne Gaol.
1892	Gold was discovered at Coolgardie in Western Australia.
1893	Australia's richest gold deposit (the 'Golden Mile') was discovered at Kalgoorlie in Western Australia.

1894	South Australia became the first Australian colony to give women the right to vote.
1895	'Waltzing Matilda' was first performed in public and *The Man from Snowy River* by Banjo Patterson was published.
1901	The six separate colonies combined to form the Commonwealth of Australia through the federation of six states under a single constitution on 1 January 1901. The first Federal Parliament met in Melbourne. Edmund Barton was the first prime minister and the national flag was flown for the first time.
	The Immigration Restriction Act was passed to restrict migration to people of primarily European origin. This became known as the 'White Australia' policy.
1902	All Australian women received the right to vote.
1908	*My Country* by Dorothea Mackellar was published.
1914–18	In 1914 the male population was less than three million. Almost 400 000 Australian troops fought in World War I and approximately 60 000 died during service.
1915	The Anzacs (members of the Australian and New Zealand Army Corps) fought against Turkish forces at the battle of Gallipoli. They landed there on 25 April 1915, and this day now commemorates all Australian soldiers who have fought in wars since then.
1920	The airline Qantas (Queensland and Northern Territory Aerial Service) was founded.
1921	Edith Cowan was the first woman elected to an Australian parliament.
1927	The federal capital was moved from Melbourne to Canberra.
1928	Charles Kingsford Smith and his crew made the first successful flight across the Pacific Ocean in the *Southern Cross*.
	Bert Hinkler made the first solo flight from Britain to Australia.
	John Flynn founded the forerunner of the modern Royal Flying Doctor Service at Cloncurry in Queensland.
1930	Phar Lap won the Melbourne Cup.
1932	The Australian Broadcasting Commission (ABC) began national radio broadcasts.
	The Sydney Harbour Bridge was completed and opened.

1939	Victoria was devastated by the Black Friday bushfires that killed 71 people.
1940	A team of scientists under Howard Florey discovered the drug penicillin.
1939–45	Australian troops fought in World War II in Europe and the Pacific region.
1945	Australia became a member of the United Nations.
	The first Sydney to Hobart Yacht Race was held.
1947	The federal government boosted the post-war European immigration program.
1948	The legendary Australian cricketer, Sir Donald Bradman, was dismissed for a duck in his final test at The Oval in London, England.
1949	Work on the Snowy Mountain Hydro-Electric Scheme began, the largest engineering project ever undertaken in Australia.
1950–53	Australian troops fought in the Korean War, as part of the United Nations force.
1956	The first television programs were broadcast in Australia by commercial stations and the ABC.
	Melbourne hosted the Olympic Games. This was the first time they were held in Australia.
1962	Australia's first commercial oil well was drilled at Moonie in Queensland.
1967	The Australian people voted overwhelmingly in a national referendum to include indigenous people in the national census.
	Ronald Ryan became the last person to be legally executed in Australia.
	Tasmania was devastated by bushfires that killed 62 people.
1965–72	Australian troops fought in the Vietnam War.
1971	Neville Bonner became the first indigenous person elected to an Australian parliament.
1972	The Governor-General dismissed the elected federal government for the first and only time in Australia's history.
1973	The Sydney Opera House was opened.
	The 'White Australia' policy of 1901 was officially dismantled.
1974	Disastrous flooding occurred in Brisbane and Darwin was ravaged by Cyclone Tracy.
1977	The Granville rail disaster killed 83 people in New South Wales.

1979	Kakadu National Park and the Great Barrier Reef Marine Park were established.
1983	Bushfires in Victoria and South Australia on Ash Wednesday (16 February) killed 71 people.
	Australia became the first foreign nation to win the America's Cup.
1988	Australia recognised 200 years of European settlement with its bicentennial celebrations.
	Australia's new Parliament House was officially opened.
1992	The Federal High Court of Australia delivered the Mabo decision, allowing indigenous native title in Australia.
1996	Uniform gun-control laws were introduced across the nation after 35 people were murdered by a lone gunman at Port Arthur, in Tasmania.
1999	A national referendum on changing the Commonwealth of Australia to a republic was unsuccessful.
2000	Sydney hosted the Olympic Games.
2002	In Bali, Indonesia, 88 Australians were killed by a bomb blast in an act of terrorism.
2003–2005	Makybe Diva won the first of three successive Melbourne Cups.
2008	A parliamentary apology was officially delivered to the 'Stolen Generation' of Aboriginal and Torres Strait Islanders, who were forcibly removed from their families in the previous century.
	Quentin Bryce became the first female Governor-General of Australia.
2009	Victoria was devastated by the Black Saturday bushfires that killed 173 people.
2010	Julia Gillard became the first female Prime Minister of Australia.

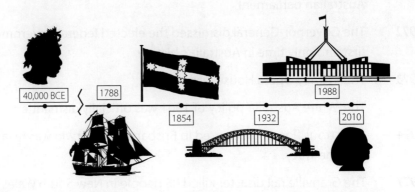

Capital Cities of the World

Country	Capital City
Afghanistan	Kabul
Argentina	Buenos Aires
Austria	Vienna
Belgium	Brussels
Brazil	Brasilia
Cambodia	Phnom Penh
Canada	Ottawa
China	Beijing
Cyprus	Nicosia
Czech Republic	Prague
Ecuador	Quito
Egypt	Cairo
Fiji	Suva
Finland	Helsinki
France	Paris
Germany	Berlin
Greece	Athens
Hungary	Budapest
India	New Delhi
Indonesia	Jakarta
Iraq	Baghdad
Ireland	Dublin
Israel	Jerusalem
Italy	Rome
Japan	Tokyo
Kenya	Nairobi
Lebanon	Beirut

Country	Capital City
Malaysia	Kuala Lumpur
Mexico	Mexico City
Morocco	Rabat
Netherlands	Amsterdam
New Zealand	Wellington
Norway	Oslo
Pakistan	Islamabad
Papua New Guinea	Port Moresby
Philippines	Manila
Poland	Warsaw
Qatar	Doha
Russia	Moscow
Samoa	Apia
Saudi Arabia	Riyadh
Solomon Islands	Honiara
South Africa	Pretoria
South Korea	Seoul
Spain	Madrid
Sweden	Stockholm
Switzerland	Bern
Taiwan	Taipei
Thailand	Bangkok
Tonga	Nuku'alofa
Turkey	Ankara
UK	London
USA	Washington DC
Vietnam	Hanoi